Watching from the Shadows

Greg Tome

Watching from the Shadows

To Norma, always and ever

Watching from the Shadows
ISBN 978 1 76041 335 4
Copyright © Greg Tome 2017
Cover photo: La Scala, Milan

First published 2017 by
GINNINDERRA PRESS
PO Box 3461 Port Adelaide 5015 Australia
www.ginninderrapress.com.au

Contents

To My Thinking Pen	7
To a Dead Mouse	9
Transfiguration: old man cooking	10
Litanous Love	11
Woman Pegging Clothes	14
Sonnet no 1	15
Concert Item: Gabriel Fauré, Elegie for Cello and Piano	16
Concert Item: John Cage, Sonata for Solo Clarinet	17
Earth Struggles Into a New Day	18
Dying Embers	19
Summer Plaint	20
Yesterday	21
The Dying of the Day	22
A Fairy Story of Our Times	23
Batting For Paradise	26
School Excursion to the NGA	28
On Turning Eighty	30
Beach Walk	31
Penny Lizard	33
Young Woman Outside La Scala	35
Filling in For Satan	37
Paranoia and Tenterhooks	42
The Voice of Shadows	46
This, Our Town	48
Impressions: Sydney Revisited	51
Questions For Mendonca	53
Anzac Heresy	57
Killing Fields	59
Memory of a Prisoner of War	61
Frank and Mark: a tribute	63

Torrington	67
New Italy New South Wales	69
Four Christmas Day Portraits	74
The Last Taxi Ride	89
One Life's Detritus	91

To My Thinking Pen

Some cord
invisible
but real
links you
when alerted
to my brain.
Along it
thoughts travel
only
    one
        way
or so I presume.
The comfort
of your snugness
between thumb
and fingers
clears the sinuses
of creativity.
What for me
are little miracles
trepid their way
to your embrace.
A happy gurgitation
leaves a tattoo
depicting their entrails
down
down
the page.

Silly words
sane words
my humble offerings
spill themselves
there
for others
to see
and puzzle
and question
their right
    to be.

To a Dead Mouse

Farewell, you night-time marauder, now caught
in the dignity of death. Can such mischief
among kitchen nectarines lead to this?
A stately picture resting demurely here,
so still on paving, accoutred in basic
gun-metal grey with pink accessories
of ears and mouth. Is this the intrepid one
who dared the cheese on trap, and won?
Like any of Livia's victims all caution gone,
one bite too many, some substance unknown
but subtly alluring brought you to this.
No funeral pyre for you, my noble little Roman.
Your little mouse eternity to be spent in landfill
covered in masses of kitchen scraps enough
to satiate your never-ending dreams.

Transfiguration: old man cooking

Today I am a creator
I measure I weigh
a little of that some of this

flour from the Germans

In the beginning was the seed

Wheat sprung from the soil, basked in the sun
stalks yielding their heads
crushed in dusty sacrifice.
Measure. Weigh. I mix
the Teutonic skill, the soil gift,
the sun basking.
I stir the slice of harvester
the carrying, the moving of flour.
Measure mix stir.
I feel the power of sun, mill, machinery
at the end of the wooden spoon.

No thought here but this
this moment is all
Buddha is in the kitchen
a miracle beckons.

And on the fourth day he created bread

Now I am a god, a minor god
my universe in a mixing bowl
my biblical script a recipe

On the next day he rested.

Litanous Love

You
My light
   my shade
My day
   my night
My dream
   my reality
My gentleness
   my strength
My zephyr
   my tempest
My hope
   my despair
My energy
   my langour
My whisper
   my rousing
My music
   my silence
My echo
   my mute
My peace
   my turbulence
My dance
   my stillness
My allegro
   my adagio

You
   only you

My reservoir
    my flood
My mountain
    my valley
My sky
    my terrain
My rainbow
    my beam
My zenith
    my nadir
My sphere
    my prism
My circle
    my tangent
My salt
    my sweetness

You
    yes, you

You
My prisoner
   my captor
My hammer
   my anvil
My sail
   my anchor
My salve
   my ache
My binding
   my unwrapping
My Paris
   my Las Vegas
My crime
   my punishment
My salvation
   my damnation
My ecstasy
   my agony
My alpha
   my omega

My all

My love.

Woman Pegging Clothes

She stands; hands as nimble
as any pianist's dance a lively jig.
Allegro molto.
Athena distributing largesse
to the faithful. Balletic grace
marking every action. Synergy of eye
and hand a delight to the watcher.
Hung garments each a sacrifice
to elegance of movement.

She returns to the house,
a goddess moving to the tabernacle.

Sonnet no 1

I send you my thoughts to be your wings
to lift you up and take you with me
to where the sun glows and breezes sing,
past troubles dim and our spirits burst free.
The chains of the dismal past chafe sore
but my dreams open up ways of escape;
the chill holding my heart begins to thaw
and a blissful future looms into shape.
But in this harbour into which we sail
the shadowy menace of rocks lie in wait.
We pray our aspirations will prevail
as past such puny threats we navigate.
Then will our love shout to split the world's ears
such as to bludgeon with joy any who hears.

Concert Item: Gabriel Fauré, Elegie for Cello and Piano

Only the cello can make that sound
that woos the stomach, drawing empathy
in visceral waves. Here it is
right at the start. The piano emerges
a respectful companion with steady
but elegant tread. An effective couple
they enmesh all in a blanket of calm
surrender before a storm breaks.
Noise and pace rage. It is an elegy
after all and complacency
is not welcome here.

But storms always pass. The cello
collects our senses, prisons them
in our entrails. The piano tactfully abets
in this exquisite bondage. There they stay
long after the music ceases.

Concert Item: John Cage, Sonata for Solo Clarinet

At last the clarinet
can sing to us unencumbered.
No rivals no need for tricky squeaky notes
to gain our attention.
Happy and relaxed she starts
with decorous greeting.
Then the music lifts her skirts
and shows her legs.
Her steps are quick and nimble
with a flash of defiance there.
A good girl at heart, she conforms,
comes back into the tent
of good manners, leaving us to wonder
why she couldn't stay longer.

Earth Struggles Into a New Day

Before dawn the first slivers of light
fight their way upward into a waiting space,
sperm competing for the egg.
For a moment the fragility of earth
is manifest in the delicate sky,
a membrane stretched tightly
over all creation. For the span
of one breath, existence is poised
on the brink.

The light strengthens, modestly at first.
A tentative confidence emerges to receive
ritual applause from expectant pennate throats.
Another day flaunts its presence –
for now earth is safe, will continue being.

Some other time
a different harm awaits it
but approaching
with certain step.

Dying Embers

The days of May bounce their heads
off the shiny bitumen roads
and then scram before the five o'clock news
finishes spewing out its parade of gloom
and paranoia, football scores
and stock market crap.
Lining the roads, those trees with the pastel-coloured leaves –
you know, the ones an exhausted creator
never got around to planting here
so we had to do it for Her –
shocked by the broadcast hysteria
they stand partly clad
as if they have just emerged
from the shower.

More pretty leaves lie fresh
at their feet. They remind me
the good times have gone
and they glow there, the dying embers
of past summer's delights and the spice
of their lingering tastes.

Summer Plaint

Summer is a flirtatious woman
plops herself down whenever it suits her
sprawling seductively over the countryside
breathing gentle breezes to win our smiles.

With darts of lightning or bellows of thunder
she punishes us when bored or angry.
Who else can raise us out of our beds
earlier than we care for? Who lures us outside
late in the evening, pricks our complacency
by teasing with insect raids? Just as quickly
she enchants by pressing against the blushing sky
a mass of birds in masterly manoeuvre
as they parade with pomp and sound
towards some distant avian Nirvana.
She keeps rain away when we want it;
delivers it when we don't. This is how
she learns who truly loves her. Another trick
is to threaten to steal away before she does.
This sort of coquetry can only last so long.

But she may well return another day.

Yesterday

When yesterday was still today I told her
that I loved her as she warmed my skin
with her smile, ruffled my hair with her sighs.
I told her that when she was still tomorrow
I had yearned for her. So why has she left me
so soon, lurching into the limbo of yesterdays?
I have known many todays. None have lingered.
All are now wrapped in the anonymity of forgetfulness
and confusion. All are time wasted, chances lost.
Just once I would like this, my last lovely yesterday
with her warming embrace and her gentle sighs
to come back to stay with me.

The Dying of the Day

Silence while the planet holds its breath.
Tall pines, gums press silhouettes
against the sky. The dying light holds
the gentle dark in a long quiet kiss.
Street lamps flicker feebly, unwilling
to take up their duties. Far above them
a sole cockatoo wonders aloud as it
searches for companions and some sense
of certainty.

The air is filled with a message beyond
our understanding but not our feeling.
Mother Earth has spun one more time;
each of us is older as this day slips beyond
our grasp. The sense of mystery lingers still.
Out there among the galaxies something
unknowable happens.

Now all is dark.

A Fairy Story of Our Times

In this land of carpets magic with beauty,
in this land where honoured traditions
stretch back into the sandstorms of time,
in this land where men with flinty hearts
have ravaged the towns, have ravaged the countryside
with their brute gluttony for power
which their dust-filled brains can't control,
in this land lived Manzoor, a dreamy gentle boy
who played and strayed far from the paths
where others clustered.

There in his dreamy gentle world Manzoor fell foul
to the brute greed of the steely men
and trod on a landmine.

Manzoor lay on the ground of this ancient land;
he lay beyond the reach of pain; he lay outside
the walls of knowing.
There he lay with his foot blown off.

Somewhere out of the evening dark,
somewhere out of the haze of the sand
blown up by the evening breeze a desert snake
tasted its way to where the boy lay
and coiled itself tightly around the damaged leg.
The snake now a tourniquet, staunching the flow of blood.

All this Manzoor knew without seeing it but knowing it
as through a prism of dream. In the self same way
he learnt that myriads of desert creatures, large and small –
mainly small, emerged from the evening dusk,
from the sand blown up by the evening breeze.

Myriads of desert creatures emerged, gathered up
Manzoor's dismembered foot. The desert creatures –
ants, scorpions, lizards – among myriads of others,
manoeuvred Manzoor's severed foot back onto his leg.

Manzoor lay on his back on the earth of the land of carpets
magic with beauty, of the land of traditions reaching back
into time, of the land ravaged by flinty-hearted men.
The join where Manzoor's foot connected to his leg
the many desert creatures – insect, lizards, birds – among others
covered with secretions gathered from special places.

A flash of lightning such as men rarely see and the desert creatures
vanished into the evening darkness, into the sand blown up
by the evening breeze. Gentle, dreamy Manzoor lay on his back
on the earth of this special land. He looked at his leg,
he looked at his foot, replaced after being blown off.
Manzoor looked at the now clear sky that seemed to smile
down at him. While his gentle dreamy heart quivered with fear
with his hands he pressed down on the earth of this special land.
Manzoor found that he could stand on his once severed foot.

There he stood and raised his arms to the sky smiling down.
He raised his arms to the tourniquet snake, the other desert creatures
now gone into the evening dark. He raised his arms for all
the gentle dreamy people who play and stray far from the paths
where others cluster, the gentle dreamy ones who lose limbs
to the brute gluttony of the men with brains of dust,
men with their hearts of flint.

Batting For Paradise

The leather orb glides from the essence,
the mathematical centre of my bat; it
bubbles across the clipped field until
caressing gently the rope, the boundary
that encircles our dreams and lives.
To err is human but this bowler does
not forgive, but yet again his alignment
is amiss. His next missile curves towards
my legs. I carve it fine to the nether regions
where the titan, resting between labours,
hurls it mightily back in our general direction.
A brace of runs for me. Eye says to hand,
'We're a good team, we are going well.'
Brain says to all, 'Don't get carried away.
Focus: just one ball at a time.' I focus.
A challenging delivery. My hopeful push
sees the ball in a space a little wide of cover.
A quick dash and I am at the other end.
'Over!' called. My partner glares at me
from his distant eyrie: I am Batman,
he Robin. I am Wooster, he Jeeves.
I smile back. I am flourishing, he scratching.
And the titan is back.
I face a thunderbolt fast short, just a little wide.
An easy swing of scythe. A loud cracking noise
like the snap of a thick tree limb –
but music to my ears.

The ball well beyond the surly bonds
of boundary ropes. A few desultory flags
are waved by the sparse beholders.
Now another thunderbolt not so short
nor quite so wide. Ah, pride goeth before
a fall, and Lord, lead us not into temptation.
With loud self-ovation the keeper snaffles
the catch. I walk the walk of the condemned.
I am as one about to mount the tumbrel.

So this is life and this is cricket
they separate and they blend
in a way that clouds my mind.
For me the grim reaper wears
an umpire's coat but needs
no referral system before he raises
the fateful finger.

So set aside the ten commandments;
leave them be to worry others.
When your time comes, simply
make sure your bat is straight
that you move your feet
but keep your head still.

After that there should be
a prime seat somewhere
in the pavilion for you
at the end of the day's play.

School Excursion to the NGA

They move from painting to painting
from gallery level to another level.
They bundle in front of different paintings,
the girls to the centre and front
the boys outliers checking regularly
as if an attack threatened.

The energy of *Blue Poles* reaches unsurely
to splash the imagination of one cluster.

Another lot puzzle sympathetically
before yielding themselves up to the magnet
of the faceless bushranger.

The warmth and order of Monet's *Haystack*
shelters a third group from the dreariness
of the day's demands.

They move from gallery level to another level
the girls bursting with confidence press
around the teacher to tell him
what he wants to hear. They embrace each other
in admiration of who they are, hands clasp,
an arm around a waist.

The boys, outliers still and still diffident,
search for different views, the special secrets
the building yields only to the curious.

*

The boys and the years will eat each other
and the years and the girls the same.
Blue Poles, *Ned Kelly* and others will become
islands in a memory of another time.

And then grown men, these boys will turn
their backs on special views granted to the few.
But threats of attack will remain and demand
above the old diffidence a shifty carapace of certainty.

These girls when women will shepherd their embraces
more carefully and discover them somewhat reserved.
Each will wonder just who she is and where
the assuredness of that distant time went.

On Turning Eighty

Like migrating birds
    like lambing ewes we learn
to sense when Mother Earth has
        sashayed once again
    completely around the sun.

Unlike the birds
    unlike the sheep
we tick them off
        these encirclements.
We number them
    the complete roundings
call them years.
        Line them up
    in rows of ten
    at finger numbers demand.

The magic of numbers
    with their strange sleight of hand
        calls to me.
Tells me on such and such a day
    (one of more numbers
boxed and filed in quirky organisation)
I will have survived
    Earth's circling sun
for eight rows
    of blocks of ten.
        Precisely

Beach Walk

The moon has pulled back the tide, a blanket
that hid a thousand secrets. New stories
are now being etched onto a blank surface,
a wide stretch of padded-down wet sand
bordering the restless surf. Footprints of walkers,
ephemeral evidence mark the sand.
Alone, or in pairs, or alone in pairs
their thoughts are embedded in marks made
as they meet or pass or greet; as they ponder
the surf playing variations on a theme; thoughts
that grow from the sight of stunted scrub,
desiccated broccoli in sour relationship
with the ungenerous rise of ridge along beach's edge.
Further back pinch-faced trees struggle to flaunt
a sense of superiority, their trunks vertical dirty
chalk lines.

The beach hieroglyphics recite their poetry defiantly
as the incoming tide bides its time.
Not all will be mopped from the record; the repeated jolt
of foot on hardened sand conducts a memory, a bonding link
between body and water, between soul and surround.

Before that, of course, there are the dogs: tethered
to their masters' hearts they prance and primp and strut
leaving all their different stories autographed behind them.
A slip from leash, a taste of freedom to wrestle the surf
an occasional privilege.

Soon enough the signs of these many bonds
will be erased; another empty canvas will wait
to collect glimpses, however fleeting, of a random array
of lives that chance scatters here
for one particular day.

Penny Lizard

As kids we called them penny lizards
    Even then perhaps
        we sensed
                their delicate dignity
their sharp little dashes
    heads held at just the right height
        to signal pride
                but not arrogance.
That's how you survive
        the
            eons.

This morning I saw one
        perform its fluid display
    pushing its way out of dry leaves
            that partner its existence.

The sight pleased me –
    here something durable
        unchanging through my long years

Before our lot emerged on land
        from the waters of darkest time
    these were long practising
        their dainty forays
    and quick double-edged scans
        for food or danger

We developed superior intellects of course
    which we've used ever since
        to batter and bash
           ideas
              each other
                  and our living spaces

Perhaps I will outlive
    this little one
        I saw this morning
But long after we have disappeared
                from the planet
having outsmarted ourselves
                into extinction
these tiny reptilian charmers
        will be here
           to dart
                and look
                    and breed
for many millennia to come.

Young Woman Outside La Scala

Light of foot she steps daintily
    entrapped in a moment of time,
    etched permanently into surroundings
    of legendary aura. Nearby La Scala
    stares with stately unperturb
    across the open space, safe
    in the knowledge the magic
    of glorious sound reassures it
    its place is justified here.

With slender elegance she steps,
    her gaze down signals her immunity
    to the tug of the glories around her
    that reach out to the rest of the world.
    But with unconscious ease she radiates
    her own offering, a sliver of healthy athleticism,
    animal-like, to complement the majesty
    of stone here and nearby where the mighty
    Milan Cathedral caresses the clear Italian sky
    in a show of enthralling strength, deceiving
    through the delicacy of the finely laced stone.

With graceful purpose she steps
    through the clear light of summer heat
    just one of many, but apart, separate
    because of some quality captured by chance
    a sense of style stamping her as belonging
    to this place, being exactly in the heart that pumps
    how this place is.

Carrying her shopping easily on her right arm
    she steps into the question:
    who is this young woman? How is she
    the focus of a photo of La Scala, a focus
    she has wrestled so effortlessly onto herself?
    Somewhere in Milan she lives, breathes, beguiles,
    not knowing a trick of fate has imprinted her
    inexorably for me as a partner of La Scala,
    of Milan class with every mention,
    every memory of there.

Filling in For Satan

Little sticks
    in the garden.
Little sticks
    in my hand.
I feed little sticks
    into this machine
        that crushes them up
            into
                tiny
                    pieces.

I feel like the devil.
In some medieval painting
    the devil feeds the souls
        the souls of the damned
            into the fires of hell.

I feel like that
    like the devil.
I like the power.
I like being the devil.

Now take this one.
This stick
   sleek
      too smooth
this stick could be
   that fatuous politician.
Into the fire
   with him.
Into little pieces
   he goes.
His glib banalities
   crushed with him.
Forever.

The next stick
   old and misshapen
      a powerful media man.
Greedy, megalomaniacal.

These ugly sticks
   his underlings
      insensitive, unscrupulous.

All of them together
   crushed.
Crushed to pieces
   in his case
      far too late.

The whole gang
    crushed
        their servile cruelty
            along with them
                for all time.

Oh I enjoy the power!
    How I enjoy
        playing the devil.
All the damned
    into the fire.
Rich and poor
    into the crushing.

But hold!
    These next sticks are dry
        thin and dry.
Where they grew
    lacked water.
They grew
    where the soil was arid.
The soil
    did not nourish.
Their bushes
    could not flourish.

For the bushes
    for the branches
        the sticks could not thrive.
Yet they are damned
    and the devil does this?
Some semblance of justice
    surely!

But where?

The book of Job
    says otherwise.

Cruel Chance
    on a high
        distant throne
gestures disdainfully.

Fate's
Kiss
Is
Random

My taste of power
    is soured.
Disillusion
    floods my veins

Game over.
    Dreaming finished.

Today
    I crush no more.

Machine
    switched
        off.

Paranoia and Tenterhooks

I tie my shoelaces
    carefully
        securely
            so I don't trip
but I mustn't waste time
Like a superannuated boy scout
    I must be ready
        any day
    one day
I'll have to move fast
    I may have to run

That's right
    for the first time
        for a long time
    I may have to run

Till then
    we live normally
        but I'm always aware
    with deer-like mentality
        sniffing the breeze
            warily
    alert to my own 9/11

I tell myself
    get your teeth clean
Could be your last chance
before the ominous phone call
    with the painful pause
        before speech
      loaded with hurt
hurt that mobilises me

I must be ready
    I will have to move fast
even think about running

Can't loiter in the shower
    a grisly news headline
hovers somewhere
    over the horizon
perhaps my own Lindt café
could come this way
    straight at us

Must be ready
I will have to move fast
    even be forced to run
Sure
    sit in the sun
        drink my coffee
    but I taste
        yawning uncertainty
    I keep my guard up

My subliminal frenzy
    I hold close
  the way a mother
      does her child
but this one is shameful
    so I hide it away
but it is there
    it is mine
      mine alone

All it takes
    is a spin of a coin
    so I always cross the road
      with good friend utmost
    then if they get me there
it will have to be
    while I'm on a zebra

this threat
    dark grey and woolly in shape
      of course
    could be for me
      me alone
    could come from within
      a fiendish mastiff
    to toy with my mind
      my memory
        or some bodily part
before shaking my life to pieces

I have to be ready
    be on my guard

I'll have to run
    no doubt about it

One day
    I'll have to run

The Voice of Shadows

A lopsided silence sits about me, perturbed by a creak of board.
A creak too slight for human agent.
Nobody is there but caused
by something unseen
perhaps unreal.

Am I watched?

A flick of shadow
haunts my perceiving.
Soon gone but I see
no bird in flight
nor moving branch leaves.

My thoughts shrivel
down passages linked
to childhood then further
further back down tunnels of time
to ancestors long gone.
Like pallid skin and rugged nose
but this, a different inheritance,
invades my outer shell of scepticism
of sane outlook.

Little glimmers from *lumen de lumine*
sift through and I feel
the shades of the dead about me.
Family, loved ones given a patrol duty
ghost of King Hamlet style
and I am on their watch.
I fear their message: a call
back to the ways
of a long yesterday.

Now I have a salvation
of a different kind. There is noise.
Any tiny creak of board cancelled
by the coarse conversation
of garden machinery.
Vetoed by a thick cloud cover
no shadows flicker.
My breathing steadies.

I view my rational thought
now a cupboard, stark, clean of line.
Practical, sensible.
But its door is shut tight.
Packed there behind it,
behind all the rational useful items lurks nagging disturbance
lurks dark and mystery.

This, Our Town

This town
    pillowed around by hills
        watching and sleeping by turns.
Cosseted by their enigmatic embrace
    the town itself sleeps,
        the streets deserts
            from an old movie.
The stillness allows
    the age of the land to peep through
        the flimsy layers
            of settlement's touch.

Scenes change briefly
    when trains
        like heedless schoolboys
    scamper past.

Forces start to nibble
    at the dominance of the night.
The earliest rays of light with endemic touch
    join hands
        with the first moving vehicles of the day.

The town now a giant's first stirrings.
Its heart pumps up the frequency of traffic,
    its entrails soon coated
        with lines
            of parked cars.

An epidemic of energy
    infects the town centre.
The people bustle about:
    sweep
hose   open
    shift
call to
    one
        another.

As the sun looms higher
    our town's heart settles
        into a quieter regular beat
    its vitality
        more carefully channelled.

Eventually
    an unacknowledged siesta sets in
        induced by a kindly glow kissing
            the shop windows
                on a favoured side of the street.

The untidy exuberance of children
    escaping the maw of school routine
        cracks open the afternoon calm.

The old town grumpily damps down
    such thoughtlessness
        begins an impatient wait
            for the entry of the gentle light
    that signals day's end.

Till then
    it settles back
        content
    for the time being
           to be
      like
  any other
      dullsburg.

Impressions: Sydney Revisited

A symphony of faces
    the people, such a lifeblood
caffeined along by mass exultation
    drawing upon the exquisite
        day's energy,
drawing upon the insistent beauty
around them which prevails
over the drab hand of commerce
    and its work.

They come in isolated groups
        in groups of isolates
    each praying into their device
plugged into their constant
    serving of inspiration.

The harbour
    the plaything of some
        whose embraces
        she brushes away
            with elegant
                disdain;
    her daunting majesty
        there for all
            but owned by none
    her warm brown
        honeycomb rocks
            timeless, sacrosanct;
    her seductive inlets crusted
        in peopled beehives
            fighting for space.

The Sydney cocktail
    spill a little;
        watch the spill spread.
There a faint trace
    of aboriginal allure.
Greed and malfeasance
        show more strongly.
A glittery but unconvincing streak
    of attempted sophistication
        dazzles briefly.
But dominating, widespread –
        not sure how deep –
    but showing up
        always there
a sense of decency,
    an appreciation
        of the value
of
    ordinariness.

Questions For Mendonca

Oh, Cristovao
    you old deceiver
in the quest for this title
    your shadow flickers only faintly
whereas the man from Ingleterra
    magicked his way
        along the difficult coast
into
    the history books
        and a nation's mythology.

The romance of your mystery bewitches
    but it's gone again
        in a flash.
You've got competition you know
    latter-day
        nothing showy there
but the carefully recorded plodding
    fuelled by the paranoia
        of the lowly birth
            of the son
    of a Yorkshire ploughman.

But who are you?
You dazzle with possibilities
    you Latin types
        with flashing smiles
and subtle hints –
    a ship way down there
        roosting among the sand hills
a set of keys
    aching of Portugal
        from the depths of lime
    – like the ship
        now gone.
Your fingerprints so ephemeral, Cristovao.

And what of your lonely cluster of ships
    battling down the never-ending coast
        picking their way against the wind
            skirting the shark-teethed coral
– or so the dream goes –
powered by sails
    shaped to honour the Trinity
        brandishing the cross of Jesus
all set to garner
    a harvest for the Pope
        of the souls of the black people
    who dissolved lilting Portuguese words
into their own tongues
    and who marvelled at the ship
abandoned in those faraway hills –
a mystery to them
as it is now to us.

The treasure to be won
>   from the so-called Isle of Gold
>   a secondary concern.

The later English mob
>   were not in the soul-saving business –
just the bodies of the Tahitian women
>   for the temporary relief
of crew far from home.
Cook wrote of the Tahitian queen's breath;
Whose breath did you sample, Cristovao?
Or did the gently sculptured face of Donna Maria
>   shadowing the recurring image of an empty nursery
>   keep you pure
>   in a Catholic
>   well-born Portuguese
>   manner?

So Captain-Major Mendonca
>   did you do all that your promoters suggest?
Such as
>   produce that map
>   of Java la Grande
>   snitched away by French agents
>   shifting you away from the spotlight
leaving you just a whisper
>   in the rustle of History's pages.

Or is the whole story a fiction
    a momentary talking point
        around the academic water cooler?
– nothing more than shadows
    cast up by a magic lantern trickster
        with an imagination similar
to that of a confident adventurous servant
    of the court of the Portuguese king
a fiction
    taken up by those impetuous to invest
        their nation's hard-edged history
            in a little more mystery
                a little more magic.

Anzac Heresy

As the leaves of trees now ours
but coming first from Mother England
begin their change of colour trick,
as the ominous breath of Autumn's dawn
chills us with a slight jolting shock,
inevitably it comes. Another Anzac Day.

They gather. At dawn they gather. So long ago,
at another dawn, those others clustered in open boats
headed towards History; many towards death
but all towards a certain immortality, an immortality
draped across a superstructure of myth which spreads
like cloud from gunfire, from bombs across the horizon
of proud Turkey.

Since then, every year across the nation
they gather. In every town, good people, sincere,
they gather. The light never dims. Those others
so long dead, so far away. Yet the light never dies.

But somewhere, far from the hobbling feet
of marching veterans, from the jaunty gait
of bright-eyed pretenders, far from the rousing music,
the speeches, the sense of wonder, the warm inner glow
another light flickers dimly sporadically. The shadows
it casts spell out different messages, words
fighting through the blanket of common sentiment:
Churchillian blunder. Now there: *led by the nose…*
Wait, something follows:…*by imperial overlords.*

So there they died, nothing gained. But the myth builds
and spreads. The futility is gilded over. The smoke and mirrors
of mindless jingoism cloud our judgement all awry. The deaths
of brave men are not seen with a clear eye. And we dodge the stark truth
by hiding behind a bonfire of delusion. The smoke blinds us.

The nation's nose remains there, poised –
ready to be led again and again into another tempting folly.

Killing Fields

The women of Srebrenica move aside
    a stranger is among them
        also searching through the bones
  A stranger
    but with their same sad eyes
  Somebody whispers
    An Egyptian goddess,
    is that possible?
Isis crosses the world
    seeks the scraps of her husband
          Osiris
  scattered
    in fourteen bits
      all over

  Some success
    but a lot more travel needed.

So many slaughter fields to visit
    their names fade from her tired mind
  Remembers some
    Kampuchea
      Auschwitz
        even somewhere called
          Myall Creek

In an exclusive club Seth
    high-fives Cain and Romulus
  surly onlookers
    Hitler, Stalin, Pol Pot
      rue the fate
      that deprived them of having brothers
      of their own to kill
Osiris will be re-gathered
    loving life breathed into him

Now big-bellied
    Isis carries within her
      dreams of a son
        Horus the living god
      whose reign will bring light,
  no matter how flickeringly brief
    for those who seek
      the bones
of
    their murdered beloved.

Memory of a Prisoner of War

He remembers
under a churlish German sky
a line of prisoners
making a road,
digging, levelling a road,
spreading metal.

He remembers
the sound of shovel scrape on metal,
the weight of metal on shovel,
his sore tired arms,
the ache below his shoulders.

He remembers the guards,
older men, bored
pondering their war
ruefully.

An old woman approached,
wrapped shabbily, shuffled
behind the guard,
stood near to him.
He remembers.

As he worked she bumped him,
with a gnarled fist, her old fist
she bumped him.
Her other hand emerged
from under a welter of cloth,
her other hand, he remembers.

A potato was proffered,
a humble potato still warm
from the oven was there,
was his for the taking.

He looked, sought her eyes
behind the limp mantle;
he nodded a thanks –
a most pitiful thanks –
he almost smiled.
He scoffed the potato.

He remembers its quick slither
of warmth, painful in the delivery
of comfort, of sensations.

The alerted guard turned,
missed her with his boot,
smacked her hip with the gun butt.
He screamed abuse.
She hobbled away
answered with curdling curses.

He plunged his shovel into the pile
of metal.
Then he knew.

She would be back;
the next day she would be there,
another potato for another prisoner.

This he remembers.

Frank and Mark: a tribute

For these men no muffled drum or gilt letters
carved in stone. Out of tune with their style,
their scorn for pomp.

Frank and Mark were brothers

They desperately clung to flotsam in a foreign sea
hopes focused on rescue, a long long way from home.
Frank and Mark drowned in the China Sea, their grave
shared by many, a fellowship stretching back in time, so far,
so very far.

Frank and Mark were my uncles

My uncles fought in the war against the Japanese.
Sons of the soil you might call them – good men
brave and strong – my uncles.

Frank and Mark my father's brothers

Prisoners of war they shouldered their shame
and worked on the railway of death.
Both were brave but Frank was strong
cared for Mark and many an other.
If they were sick Frank gave his food
worked their shift. A special man was Frank.

Frank and Mark fond uncles of many

I remember the day the sad news came
Frank and Mark drowned in the China Sea.
I remember the quiet; even the boards
of the old house where they had lived
dared not creak a sound. No word was spoken.
No sense was there
in a world without Frank and Mark.

Frank and Mark shared a grave in the China Sea

So many joined them, in a short few days,
their bodies wafted by currents below the surface
a mirror of life forces, of chance that took them
here and there – the water enriched in liquid lives
by the lives of so many.

Frank and Mark drowned with so many others

An old man facing the end of his days – decades, decades later,
Frank's memory lived in his head, he saw Frank's face;
in his head he saw Frank's strong face, an Italian face.
He heard his words, clear tough strong words. In his head
he heard Frank's words again. He tells a nurse.

Frank and Mark an old man remembered them

'Don't you die, you wretch. Don't let the bastards win.
You will live. You'll be home again. Don't you ever give in.'
Frank's words he tells to the nurse, a woman
linked to the family of Frank and Mark.

Frank and Mark worshipped by an old dying man

They survived the railway of death, their prize
a trip to Nippon to work in a factory there.
A ship was to take them to the Land of the Rising Sun.

Frank and Mark boarded the Rakuyo Maru.

Down in the holds of this doomed ship
crowded together in the fetid dark
they waited and wondered, some feared.
No red cross signalled its special cargo
and the Americans sank it fierce.

Frank and Mark floated there under a tropical sky

The torrid sun beat down on the sons of the soil
lives lived long from the sea.
They clung to timber, they clung to hope,
kept their heads above the surface
of the always-hungry mighty China Sea.
'Don't give in. Stay awake. There'll be rescue soon.'

Frank and Mark called to each other as they floated in the China Sea.

Two long days waiting; floating with them
faces they loved, images of home
of friendly sloping hills, of grey bushland.
They waited for rescue. Rescue so slow coming.
Then Frank was gone and the next day Mark
slipped away into the sea. So much more water
than they had ever known.

Frank and Mark sank into the sea.

Rescue came. The Americans came
but Frank and Mark had gone.
Those still afloat were saved.
Some looked at where their dead friends
had been and wondered
at the way fate works.

A sad story repeated in mankind's long saga
the good die and the unjust thrive
just as the Book of Job says,
and those of us left ponder
the twisted way life on the old Earth works.

Frank and Mark live on for us
fortunate few who know their story.
Soon enough it too will fade
and disappear with them
beneath the waters of time.

Torrington

Despite its name no market town in Devon is this place.
More a hideout where only the blousy old pub flaunts
its up-yours presence. Other dwellings shrug away
their existence, crouching close to the ever-present bush,
while granite boulders, randomly placed by a bored God,
obscure the path taken by the white dusty road.
The village itself shelters into the wilderness
of wooded ranges as far from the world as it can get.

And here for me it all began, this teaching lark.
I lived at the pub, went to a stone church
once in a while; loved the landlord's wife
from a great distance – I'm sure she guessed.
At the end of my time there she took my hand,
held it for so long it brought a blush that
nearly caused my nineteen-year-old ears to burst
into flames. Wrote to me sometimes. But I digress.

I remember my first day teaching, little blonde Linda
welcomed me with a vomit quite close
to my carefully polished shoes.

Weekends spent exploring the bush with others, a rifle
or two, tin cans our only target – no animals
were hurt in the writing of this poem –
rocks down the mining shafts for wolfram
taking an eternity to hit bottom.
Even the metal ore hid deep away
from the world of others.

      As did the old men,
distorted successors of the anchorites of old,
with rare appearances out of nowhere, their dog
and sugar bag of metal ore, its worth soon drunk.
Back to the wilds again with sugar, tea, flour –
these silent men who saved their talk
for their dog, or themselves when alone.

I remember the kids' gossip eliciting
some gentle advice from the headmaster
because I walked home for lunch each day
accompanied by Gloria, the butcher's daughter.
Such a mild indiscretion, and so long ago.

Where now is Gloria, little Linda, or landlord's wife
or the hawk-eyed headmaster with the generous
heart? Time swallows us all bit by bit, until
only God's careless granite rocks will remain.

New Italy   New South Wales

Such trees were there
not so much to greet them
as to watch their arrival
watch disdainfully their apprehensive arrival.
Great virile strange trees different
from those in the measured fields
of northern Italy different
from the menacing jungle
of that fetid swamp
that island Nouvelle France
that a French marquis
with the lupine eyes tricked them to buy.
Their new Jerusalem, their slippery dream
of a bountiful future.
Their tropical hell.

This was a better place.

The trees were not friendly nor harmful
just silent onlookers passive sentinels
as the newcomers huddled
in their family groups in tents
or hasty lean-tos.

At night there was time
the days were hard but at night
still there was time while the axes
were being resharpened
while aching backs were
being rubbed by loving hands
with the gentle accompaniment
of words of praise of words of hope
time to talk, time to remember
the landlord's agent's voice
loaded with contempt
remember the endless chug
of the crowded ship's engine.
There was time to remember the funerals
in Nouvelle France; death from malaria
death from starvation death from despair

Time to remember the deaths at sea
when desperation drove them to Noumea.
No priest now. There had been desertions.
What else would you expect from a priest
chosen by the marquis? Two captains gone.
Those left did not have the strength to hate
those who abandoned them.

At night after the talk comes sleep;
with sleep come dreams.
Morning brings waking,
but just before waking you remember them,
the dreams – replays of those other episodes.
They sink away as your tired body aches,
your bones ache, you ache again to be back at work,
another day battling those trees
trees that have to be felled,
battling the harsh ungiving soil
that has to be tilled.
But the dream replays are always there
in the cockpit of your brain.
A hair trigger is touched
the replays start again.

Desperate times in Noumea
bargaining with the French
being offered equality
with their wretched convicts.
But somehow Sydney beckoned –
an impossible dream
but not if everything was sold
even the ships as well,
the ships now almost their homes.
Now they had nothing,
just the passages to Sydney
for everybody.

In Sydney hands were generous:
food shelter clothes
medicine kind words advice.
Generous hands indeed.
But what of the hearts, what of the eyes?
Can such kindness lead to heartbreak?
After all the shared suffering, the hesion,
the herence, the sticking together by sweat,
by blood, the seepage from wounds
by hot salty tears, by sharing the last breaths
of dying loved ones
they were separated, scattered, dispersed
to here, to there, to wherever.
Until this.

They were given land.
Here, given by a man with a thick white beard
through which he spoke with an English dialect
a kindred soul who had known hardship himself
driven to seek salvation on these very shores.
The scattered regathered as if drawn
by a compelling thread. Regathered here.

Truly this was a better place.

Then came others, many neighbours
from the old northern villages.
Here among the aloof trees the air resonant
with such names:
Ballistuzzi Mellare Piccoli
Morandini Capelin Catalano
Pezzutti Scarabelloti.
And on the lips of their sweethearts
Guidetta Giovanna Caterina Zelinda.

This was a better place.

In time this special colony grew
it laboured, it loved it argued.
Some families thrived, others struggled.
Soon leaving became inevitable.

Wherever they went the bloodstream
of a new nation eagerly dissolved
the gift of their talents, their energy.
Today a museum, a memorial mark
their story, a story still best known
by the silent, watchful trees.

Four Christmas Day Portraits

Vincent

Vincent ponders Christmas Day
    seeping over the landscape
        of midwinter Arles.
Before a reluctant sun
    climbs into an unhelpful day
        a trip to the *boulangerie*
Payment
    a sketch of a fence
        grudgingly accepted –
            an act of seasonal generosity
the sketch's charm climbs
        out of the shabbiness
            of the creased paper.
Afterwards, sparsely peopled roads
    see his figure
        hunched against the chill wind
      his gait a protest
        against the low grey sky
            the lack of summer colour.

*

Carefully nursing in his paint-cracked hands
                his glass of essential comfort
                              he sits alone
    His only communication
                in the sad light of the bar
                      is a rare brief nod
        an acknowledgement of his existence
                          nothing more

He nurses his loneliness
                as carefully as his absinthe.
            Loneliness is who he is.

He aches the hours towards tomorrow
                when he will take up easel and canvas
            to defy the cruel breeze
                      from the distant sea
                and lure into existence
                      memories from summers past.

Napoleon

Napoleon has a burr in his pants
   he bustles about
         abhors these days of indolence.
   What is the purpose of it all?
     Why are we sitting about
            doing nothing?
   The supposed birthday of someone
           who never led an army
              let alone create an empire.
   Why did Alexander and Julius miss out?
   And now him?

The feast of the assumption of the Virgin into Heaven
     nestles on his birthday
        a much better reason
           for celebration and sloth
              if there has to be one.

Josephine, of course, is caught up
        in the whole mindless merry-go-round
    Ever the anti-virgin
        she delays his taking breakfast
            insisting they recognise the day
      by what turned out to be
        a most unsatisfactory exchange
            of mutual grapplings

which only angers him more
      as he glowers over breakfast
        sumptuous
           perfect in all respects
    but he
        anxious to find fault
           lets the frustration
                unedge his appetite.

                *

Now the thoughtless woman
                gushes welcomes to an array of guests
      He shows no warmth in acknowledging them
        nobody here of any use to him
           freeloaders all
                he wishes he could legislate
                    out of existence.

    He struts about
        takes his leave

So many mirrors
        here in the Tuileries
he likes his image
    but a bit taller
        would suit him
He might concede Christ
        superiority there
    but only in that.

He notes the great hallways
        empty of people today
he prefers crowds
    moving purposefully
        the source of advice
            the carrying out of orders
                messages.
Today they are elsewhere
        guzzling
            sleeping

He looks for soldiers
        the protectors of his person
worries that they be infected
    by the laxity of the day
He remembers the attempts
        to kill him –
    the memories sear.
He barks orders
    for a wide-awake sentry
        outside his office door.

*

He sits at his desk
    tapping his teeth
        with the end of his pen
Laughs aloud
        but to himself
    In the land of shopkeepers
        Cromwell half did it
Could he
        the mighty emperor
            with one scratch of his pen
        abolish Christmas
            altogether?

Well
    perhaps
        not yet.

Cassandra

    Cassandra shrugs herself
        tightly into her shawl
    squirms into the only nook
        that allows entry to the late-rising sun
    Bemoans her old bones surrender
        to the cold.
    Henry is coming
        to take her to dinner
    so no fire is lit.
    There is no coal in the cottage.
        Later Henry will bring some up
            from the cellar.
    Henry, the family angel
        her oxygen.

Misery of body leads misery
        into her head.
She laces her wait
    with a review of an invoice
        of family deaths.
    First in her head
        always first
            her sister Jane
        dearest friend Jane
            meeting death in her arms
                Jane

Others of course
> her poor Thomas
>> her parents
>> her sister-in-law
> now replaced
>> inadequately
>>> to say the least

Her mother
> her namesake
>> dead recently
but Jane rules memory
Jane her kindred
> the writer
she the illustrator
> partners in their own particular mischief
Sadness fuddles her brain
> clears at the sound
>> of wheels on gravel.
> Henry is here.

*

Eleanor the young wife
> Henry's second
>> presides
her aloofness
> enough to congeal the gravy
>> coating the mutton leg.

In return, for Jane's sake
    Cassandra spurns her
        silently
As ever, Henry's glib tongue smooths
            the day
    Calculated bonhomie for dessert.

Then, as certain
    as the cramped afternoon
        will fade
    the conversation turns to Jane
      their darling sister
        the joy of readers everywhere
Since her death
    her fame has grown
        two more novels published.

Meanwhile Eleanor turns villain
        exploits her own special genius
           against Jane's memory
    Denigrates without seeming to to move her lips
    Cassandra senses each subtle jibe
        each stamped on her heart
           painfully
consoles herself with the thought
        such a celebration of the season
           of joy and good will
    would have delighted Jane
        grist for her mill

But the scars stay
        Cassandra will re-visit them
                painfully
                      often.

*

A lifetime of Jane's letters
      gossip on the table beside her
Cassandra considers the fire
            that Henry lit.

    Now the letters

Cassandra culls out the respectable
               suitable for probing strangers
      after she has gone
         to seek out her sister
            in another world.

The others
            the scurrilous
    the funny   the impertinent
      so much my real Jane
        not for others
    not for the haters, the hurters
      the ignorant
           the Eleanors
      but mine
           mine alone
      They die with me.

The little coal fire
        flares up
    as it consumes
        sheet by sheet
            the wit
the style   the secret
        the love
    All done

Cassandra slumps back
        in her chair
    as if preparing for her own demise
        that can't be long coming
    for a time of reaching out
        dead to dead
    from St Nicholas churchyard, Chawton
to
    Winchester Cathedral
        as only Jane would understand.

The mother

The words of the sermon
   wrapped in a brogue
      evaporate in the air
            inside the hot little box of a church

Reluctantly she gives up on the sermon
   allows a host of competing thoughts
      to wash through her brain.
She feels the wriggles
      of her youngest
          her only daughter
     pressing against her side
        fighting the oppression
           of being confined
Four sons fill the remaining bench space
      willingly enough
          for a given time
No husband, no eldest son –
   engorged by the maw of war
Her housewifely shoulders
       bear the demands
         of farm
          of family
Demands
   like dust from a paddock being ploughed
     flurry about her
        tyre rationing   clothes
  coupons   grocery bills
    wheat harvest

Brothers-in-law
        helpful always
    give cagey advice
but the muscle, the work
    must come from the bones
              of teenage sons
      surrendering their youth unstintingly
        at the feet
            of the most demanding necessity

Ite missa est
    Go the Mass is finished
She contemplates
      the journey home
            packed into the Vauxhall
    consuming petrol
        wear on tyres
the driver
    legal
        but under age

*

A black Orpington, Eva
                is the casualty of Christmas
Scalded,
      her lifeless body
                yields up her feathers
Her separated head
        a plaything
               thrown one to another
                      by the spirited sons
Transformed in the oven
              her skin impeccable
                      glowing with allure
The sons don't linger
          over Eva's charms
There is work awaiting
              the harvest to be finished
Scuttlebutt outside the church
              wheat ripening quickly
                    urgent need to collect the grain –
      not a moment to be wasted
    They prepare
muted excitement
          at what is expected
      diluted by dread
             the thought of ache and exhaustion
She presides at their departure
              her heart battering
                      her throat's base

*

All her children sleep
    her empty bed waits in vain
        no place for one
              with head gyrating
                      with thoughts
                body tense with worry
She smokes
    a silly futile act
She never smokes
        except now
            the loneliest emptiest hours
So much to do
    such desperate need
        for her soulmate
    A yawning emptiness
        in her whole existence
An end to all this?
        Those flat never-ending plains
            she has seen out west
    she sees one now
        stretching –
            stretching
The horizon so far away
    has no relevance.
    Thus she sees her future.

The Last Taxi Ride

Oh, glum chauffeur,
nobody is bustling to head the line at that rank
where you collect your fare.
But as my years spin by in a dizzy cycle
of days and weeks I move closer
to the front of that fatal queue.
Not there yet and in no hurry
but I glimpse too often in my idle thoughts
a distinctive vehicle, a sedan smelling of finality
cruising with cold menace, testing out the terrain
around where I live.

Occasions once much celebrated shock me
with their rapid return. The question beckons
Will there be such another? For me, that is.
All others, the great grey mass of humanity
will continue celebrating this and that
never noting that I, a flyspeck
on the edge of our shared togetherness
will have gone, careering off, strapped tightly
into this conveyance where each one day
must take a final journey.

Well, gruff pilot, I ask myself what style of journey
awaits me. No flights of angels will sing me to my rest.
That is not your company's style. More like
a sharp sudden dash, perhaps with a touch
of thief in the night stuff. There are other options –
a slow drawn out process, pain and all thrown in.
Could I bear this? My God, we would be sick of each other
by the time it was over, a ridiculous journey
fuelled by that special hospital smell,
the clang of trolleys, voices hovering
just above my level of awareness,
earnest voices, friendly voices
but out of my reach. Haze, confusion and fear, endless tests
you can't prepare for – false hopes
set against the gritty reality, a reality
I would know too well and could not alter.

Too much confusion, such bother is left behind;
spare them, my close ones, a long grinding wait as well.
Give me the Business Class passage and make it quick.
But most of all, I beg you, I almost pray, let me leave
with dignity, at least a few shreds of dignity. Dignity.
Do you know the word? Or doesn't it fit easily
with that taxi loitering there somewhere outside?

One Life's Detritus

In memory of Ann
Aged 47 years

Such simple words. A life reduced
to such words lined in stone.
All that love
reduced to this;
companionship over decades
reduced to this;
heartaches, sorrows, joys
reduced to these nineteen words
weathered in stone
by the arrogance of time.

Beloved Wife of George

Yet there is more.
Away from our eyes
contained in the best local timbers
bones and dust in that capsule
somewhere below the stone words
a distillation of so much.
Powder once flesh on arms grasped
by so many friends. Bones
once arms that encircled George –
her loving George.

Died 23 March, 1883

Flesh now dust: flesh once
stroked, caressed, held,
irrigated by blood quickening
at the sound of his footfall.
All these, so much has filtered down
to this, a small space in a small forgotten place.

Thy Will Be Done

www.ingramcontent.com/pod-product-compliance
Lightning Source LLC
Chambersburg PA
CBHW062139100526
44589CB00014B/1629